My First

Picture Alphabet

Award Publications Limited

4 - 2014

ISBN 978-1-84135-522-1

Copyright © 2008 Award Publications Limited

Illustration and design by Heather Kirk

First published 2008

Published by Award Publications Limited,
The Old Riding School, The Welbeck Estate,
Worksop, Nottinghamshire, S80 3LR

www.awardpublications.co.uk

11 3

Printed in China

Aa

aeroplane

ant

anchor

apple

acorn

apron

astronaut

B b

bell

boy

ball

balloon

bread

bowl

banana

book

butterfly

Cc

candles

clown

cake

clock

cat

cup

cushion

carrot

crocodile

Dd

doll

duck

dolphin

drum

dinosaur

digger

dog

Ee

egg

Earth

elephant

envelope

eggcup

Ff

fork

flowers

fairy

fish

Gg

glass

gate

goat

girl

gorilla

grapes

goldfish

Hh

helicopter

hammer

heart

honey

handbag

hen

Ii

insect

ice cream

igloo

island

Jj

jug

jam

jewel

Kk

kettle

key

knife

knot

kitten

kite

L l

lamp

lamb

lemon

log

leaf

lollipop

ladder

lion

Mm

milk

moon

mouse

mittens

mushroom

mug

mop

monkey

Nn

net

newspaper

nest

nose

Oo

orange

owl

octopus

Pp

pear

peas

present

puppy

potato

paint

penguin

paintbrush

Qq

queen

quilt

Rr

rocket

rainbow

rabbit

robot

S s

spoon

star

sheep

scooter

T t

teapot

tomato

tractor

tortoise

U u

unicorn

uniform

umbrella

V v

violin

vulture

vase

Ww

whale

window

watch

Xx

xylophone

x-ray

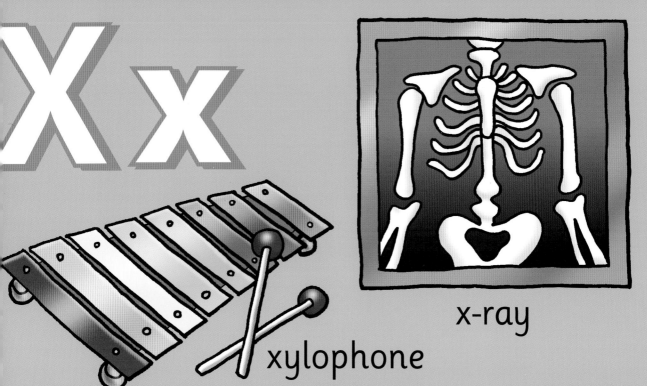

Yy

yo-yo

yogurt

yacht

Zz

zebra

zip

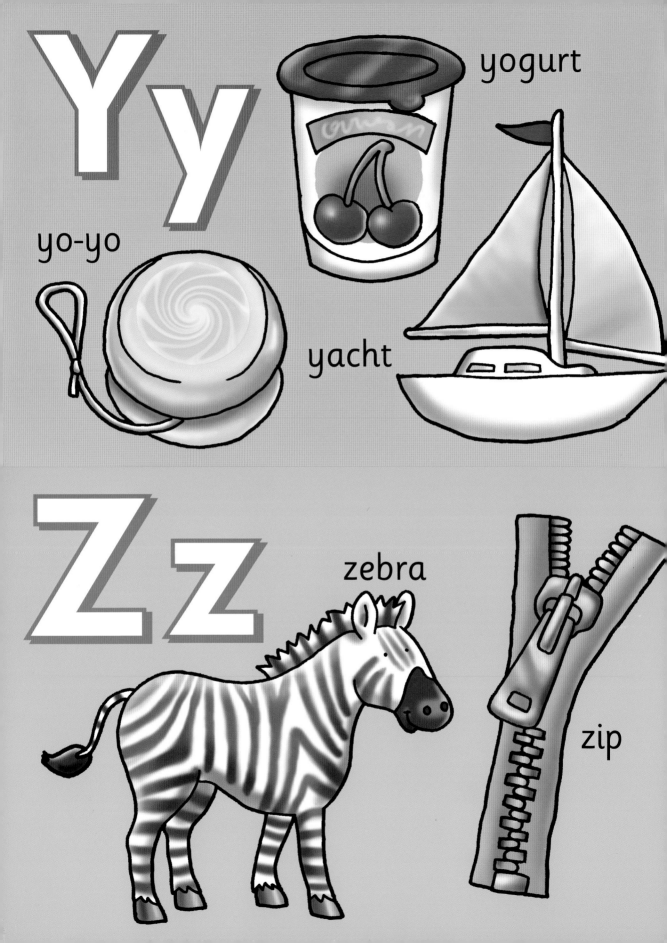